Goldie
The Two-Horned Unicorn

Written and Illustrated by
TiaMarie Arnold

Copyright

**Goldie the Two-Horned Unicorn
copyright © 2020 by TiaMarie Arnold**

Illustrated by TiaMarie Arnold

There once was a two-horned unicorn who was shiny and bright. Her mane was golden and her smile would light up the night.

Goldie was her name and she was young and free. She never knew a stranger, she was friendly as could be. Every time Goldie smiled her two horns shined bright. They made her sparkle like gold, it was such a beautiful sight.

Goldie really loved to sing and animals would stop and cheer. Birds would sit and listen in awe of her beautiful musical ear. Goldie had a favorite song that she would always sing. "I am happy as can be that it makes my voice ring. I am happy can't you see? Will you join me and sing?"

She would sing and gallop through the fields with no fear in sight. All of her animal friends would follow her sparkle with great golden delight.

Every day was a day of play and extravagant make-believe. She went on adventures to beautiful castles, and carnivals, and even sailing across oceans and seas!

**Goldie had never met other young unicorns,
she thought she was the only one. Her two
horns never bothered her at all, Goldie just
wanted to have fun.**

One day, Goldie's mom allowed her to
cross over the bridge to explore.
What she found on the other side was way more
than she had bargained for.

She met other young unicorns but they were not the same. They all were very different from Goldie with only one horn crowning their mane. They looked at Goldie with much disgust and some were even rude and mean. It made Goldie feel ashamed and it hurt her self-esteem.

10

Goldie's special horn began to shrink because she wouldn't smile. And, as time continued on it completely disappeared after a while. Goldie wasn't shining and her song was no more. She was losing her sparkle and her desire to gallop and explore.

She now looked like the other young unicorns but that didn't bring her joy. Goldie was no longer made fun of but her self-esteem was completely destroyed.

While crossing over the bridge one day she heard an amazing thing. A song of joy, a song of cheer, and a song she used to sing. "I am happy as can be that it makes my voice ring. I am happy can't you see? Will you join me and sing?' She began to follow the joyful voice as it grew louder and louder.

14

She came upon a Sparkling Red Bird who was singing under a beautiful flower. He sang, "I'm a Sparkling Red Bird who loves to sing. I'm a Sparkling Red Bird with only one wing."

Goldie gasped and her eyes grew big - this bird had an amazing difference! Yet, even though he was odd and unique he still sang with joy and persistence.

Sparkling Red Bird boldly asked Goldie why she looked so mad. "I'm not mad" Goldie exclaimed, "I'm just extremely, extremely sad."

He listened to her story but became quite confused. "You mentioned two horns," he said, "But when I look, I only see one - not two. What happened to your other horn?" he asked. "Where did it go?" She told him it went away because she didn't want it to show.

Sparkling Red Bird felt sad for Goldie and wanted to cheer her up. So he began to sing their song again hoping it would lift her spirits up. He started to sing.

Goldie started to smile. Her light began to shine. She listened and hummed and listened some more, then joined in on the last line.

Goldie began to sing on her own and suddenly her second horn began to grow! She sang the last word with so much joy...

that golden sparkles burst from her fur and began to glow! "Whoa! What was that?" Sparkling Red Bird asked. "It was the most beautiful thing!" But Goldie froze in embarrassment because it was the first time her gold ever burst when she let her voice ring.

Sparkling Red Bird loved Goldie's two horns; he encouraged her to remain unique. "Goldie you look beautiful," he said, "and you're glowing as we speak." Goldie looked at Sparkling Red Bird and said, "You know what? You're right! My two horns are what make me Goldie. It's my job to be Golden and to shine bright.

If you can have joy and sparkle with one wing, then I can be a two-horned unicorn, shine bright, and sing! I will never try to be an ordinary unicorn again because that's not who I am."

**From that day forward Goldie was proud of
her two horns, and she shined golden
throughout the land!**